AMERICAN ESSAYS IN LITURGY 9

SERIES EDITOR, EDWARD FOLEY

POPULAR CATHOLICISM:
A HISPANIC PERSPECTIVE

ARTURO PÉREZ

D0646191

The Pastoral Press
Washington, D.C.

ISBN 0-912405-58-9

The Pastoral Press is the publications division of the National
Association of Pastoral Musicians, a membership organization
of musicians and clergy dedicated to fostering the art of musical
liturgy.

Printed in the United States of America

Acknowledgments

The National Pastoral Plan for Hispanic Ministry uses the term pastoral de conjuncto, meaning that Hispanic ministry is co-responsible and collaborative. This work is one small example of this "conjunto." I am grateful for the collaboration and advice of Sr. Rosa María Icaza CCVI of the Mexican American Cultural Center in San Antonio and Sr. Ana María Pineda SM of Chicago's Catholic Theological Union. I am also deeply appreciative to José López for his fine translation. Un fuerte abrazo de agradicimiento is extended to my editor, Edward Foley, whose remarkable patience, encouragement, and talents will surely win him a place in heaven.

A. P.

CONTENTS

INTRODUCTION

Life is basically simple. It is a time of laughter and tears, memories and new experiences, encounters with God and with the devil. Life is basically simple. Our grandparents—ancestors by another name—knew and know this truth. They teach it to us in many different ways.

A Traditional Creation Story[1]

In the beginning, after God created the wonderful skies, the marvelous clouds and wind, and had placed the beautiful moon, stars, and sun in their place, he turned his attention to the earth. He made it rich and happy when he raised up the mountains, carved out valleys, plowed the rivers and lakes, and placed a multitude of animals, fish and birds to run, swim and fly over and through this creation. Having done all this, he sat down early one morning under a palm tree and felt good . . . but all alone.

Inspired by his creation, God crawled out from under the palm and dug into the dirt, molding and shaping a new form of life. Finishing the form, he spat onto it and crawled back under the palm to wait for the sun to do its work. But waiting, when you are alone, goes by ever so slowly. Anxious to see his creation, God moved out to unveil what he had done. Blowing and dusting off the dirt, a man stood up, white and fresh. He quickly started hopping around because his sensitive feet found the dirt too hot. A puzzled God led his dancing friend to the shade of the palm tree.

After becoming acquainted with his new creation, God was not quite pleased with what he had done, and decided to try again, so he crawled on all fours and again dirtied his hands in the shaping of a new friend. Soon the molding and spitting was done. By now the sun was at its peak, very bright and hot. God returned to the palm tree and his first friend, and was soon caught up in easy conversation. Suddenly God remembered, "O man! It's been so long." Running to the special place, he quickly blew off the dirt and dusted off the man who appeared straight and tall and very, very black before him. "Marvellous," God thought, and led him to the tree to be introduced to his other companion.

By now the mid-afternoon breezes were beginning to stir, signaling that evening was not far away. God thought, "One more time." Crawling, shaping and spitting was now the pattern, but this time patience and attention were added. More time than the first but less time than the second were the thoughts of this afternoon. Standing in front of this effort, God carefully dusted off his friend who now stood before him—a glorious brown in color." This is good . . . perfect!" was the satisfied sigh of God. He led this new creation back to the palm and introduced him to his companions. Then the four sat beneath the palm to watch the sun set and enjoy the evening together.

We are all shaped and molded by our families, our traditions and our stories. This is how we come to know life from a certain perspective. Attitudes and values are learned and handed down as part of our cultural inheritance. The way we view the world enables us to make decisions about how to live from one day to the next and more basically motivates us to simply get up each morning. The creation story quoted above is one Hispanic perspective not only about the way the world began, but also about why we keep going. **Appreciation** is a key concept here: appreciation for the world which was lent to us by a good and gracious God; appreciation for other people, different from ourselves yet formed by the same dirt and same loving hand of our creator; and appreciation for the place our grandparents and ancestors hold in our families for their life-giving wisdom.

Appreciation clearly extends to religious as well as cultural traditions. Together these shape the way we live, share a meal with our family, or bring a loved one to final rest. It is this perspective which we bring to our faith: a broadening point of view which assures us that prayer does not demand a special building. The church as God's people, as baptized followers of Jesus, does not need to be confined within four walls in order to worship. Prayer flows from the heart anywhere and in any place. Four consecrated church walls are good: as good as the four walls consecrated by family life called home, where prayer is also shaped and molded. It is within this perspective that the Hispanic church flowers. Here we understand that parish life and home life, official prayer and home prayer, liturgy and popular religiosity are not opposed—but rather form a unity of worship and praise.

Certainly this is in keeping with the ancient tradition of the church. Christianity, in its worship and preaching, was from the beginning inclusive, flexible, and adaptable. Thus Chupungco notes:

> ... adaptation to various cultures has been a constant feature of Christian liturgy. Indeed, it is part and parcel of her tradition. The apostles did it, and so did the Fathers of the Church and her pastors far into the Middle Ages. Adaptation of the liturgy to various native genius and tradition is not a novelty but fidelity to tradition.[2]

The Constitution on the Sacred Liturgy, the great liturgical declaration of Vatican II, supports this presumption of adaptation when it notes that "the church has no wish to impose a rigid uniformity in matters which do not involve the faith or the good of the whole community. Rather she respects and fosters the spiritual adornments and gifts of the various races and peoples." (#37) This is unquestionably reminiscent of an earlier time marked by inclusivity, flexibility, and adaptability.

The Latin American Episcopal conferences of Medellin, Columbia (1968) and Puebla, Mexico (1979) harmonize with the Constitution on the Sacred Liturgy when they call for incarnating "the true and authentic spirit of the liturgy within the Latin American reality." In the document *Pastoral de Masas* from the conference of Medellin we hear:

> Without breaking the bruised reed or extinguishing the smoking flax, the Church accepts with joy and respect, purifies and incorporates into her deposit of faith the diverse "religious and human elements" hidden in this religious sense as "seeds of the

Word" knowing they constitute, or could constitute an evangelical preparation. (#5)

Eleven years later, the conference of Puebla continued and further developed this train of thought in the document *La Evangelización en el Presente y en el Futuro de América Latina:*

> Private prayer and popular piety, present in the soul of our people, constitute evangelization values. The liturgy is the privileged moment of communion and participation for an evangelization that leads to integral, authentic Christian liberation. (#895)

These conferences were quite realistic in their approach and reflected a maturity of judgment which allowed them to recognize the positive elements of popular religiosity. At the same time, however, these documents clearly warn against those syncretistic and superstitious tendencies which would inhibit the development of the Hispanic community and tend to isolate it from the wider church.

Pope Paul VI similarly expressed care and caution for what he calls "popular piety" in his apostolic exhortation *On Evangelization in the Modern World.* His words are well worth remembering:

> Popular religiosity of course certainly has its limits. It is often subject to penetration by many distortions of religion and even superstition. It frequently remains at the level of forms of worship not involving a true acceptance by faith. It can even lead to the creation of sects and endanger the true ecclesial community.

> But if it is well oriented, above all by a pedagogy of evengelization, it is rich in values. It manifests a thirst for God which only the simple and poor can know. It makes people capable of generosity and sacrifice even to the point of heroism ... it involves an acute awareness of profound attributes of God ... (and) it engenders interior attitudes rarely observed to the same degree elsewhere. (#48)

Few have so eloquently or succinctly summarized the potential strengths and weaknesses of popular religiosity. Thus these

4

words should never cease to encourage and caution us in the pastoral work before us.

From this side of the creation story, appreciation becomes a simple act whereby we express our gratitude for what we have been given. Being Mexican American, the author acknowledges a certain bias, not in preference of but rather having more familiarity with the traditions of Mexico. Having served the Puerto Rican community for many years and being associated with other Hispanic groups, however, has enabled me to grow in appreciation of the richness in diversity that characterizes the Hispanic community. Such appreciation moves us toward one another, allows us to recognize the same creative hand in each other's culture, and enables us to establish bonds of affection and peace. Thus we are privileged to see our life in a new way: as part of a single and wonderful creation.

DEFINITION AND ORIGIN OF POPULAR RELIGIOSITY

Comments at the Rectory Door

"We don't do those things here; we only baptize the baby."

"Customs like that are superstitious, and they should be eliminated."

"When will these people learn that they're in America, and they should follow American customs."

"Your parish is Our Lady of Guadalupe. Go over there, where they'll understand what you want!"

For the longest time popular religious customs have been misunderstood, denigrated, and even banned from mainstream church life. These *religious acts* are not recorded in books or outlined in well accepted theories, but are lived out in the lives of people. Often, however, they are treated as pagan acts of a primitive and unenlightened people. They have thus become another obstacle to communication between one group and another, provoking fear of the unknown, and sometimes fostering attitudes of prejudice and discrimination.

Within the Hispanic community feelings of rejection, embarrassment, and anger arise. Perhaps enough experiences like these and the implicit message to "go away" could have been taken to heart by our people, but such was not the case. The Hispanic community confronted with closed church doors did not leave the church. Yet, they continued to be fed by their popular religious customs which nourished a relationship with the God they knew and loved.

6

As the church is coming to realize, such religious acts, so deeply rooted in the culture, cannot be ignored or suppressed without inflicting serious damage on the entire religious consciousness of a people. Popular religiosity is not a fad or something extraneous to a people but, as the conference of Puebla defined it:

> By religion of the people, popular religiosity or popular piety we mean the whole complex of underlying belief rooted in God, the basic attitudes that flow from these beliefs and the expressions that manifest them. It is the form of cultural life that religion takes on among a given people. In its most characteristic cultural form, the religion of the Latin American people is an expression of the Catholic Faith. It is a people's Catholicism. (#444)

The shapes and forms of such "popular Catholicism" vary from people to people. In the Latin American community the

> forms . . . are quite diverse, and they are both communal and personal in character. Among them we find the cultic worship of the suffering, crucified Christ; devotion to the Sacred Heart; various devotions to the Most Blessed Virgin Mary; devotion to the saints and the dead; processions; novenas; feasts of patron saints; pilgrimages to sanctuaries; sacramentals; promises; and so forth. (#912)

While recognizing the positive aspects of these customs, however, the church has also keenly recognized that there are potential difficulties with popular religiosity.

> Popular piety represents such positive aspects as a sense of the sacred and the transcendent; openness to the Word of God; marked Marian devotion; an attitude for prayer; a sense of friendship, charity, and family unity; an ability to suffer and to atone; Christian resignation in irremedial situations; and detachment from the material world. (#913)

> But popular piety also presents negative aspects; lack of a sense of belonging to the Church; a divorce between faith and real life; a disinclination to receive the sacraments; an exaggerated estimation of devotion to the saints, to the detriment of knowing Jesus Christ and his mystery; a distorted idea of God; a utilitarian view of certain forms of piety; an inclination, in some

places, toward religious syncretism; the infiltration of spiritism, and in some areas, of Oriental religious practices. (#914)

This mixture of positive and negative tendencies is more understandable when one considers the historical evolution of these customs. The conquest of Mexico and of all Latin America is a story of politics and religion, of the cross and crown. Eyewitness accounts depict Indian martyrs dying faithful to their traditional beliefs rather than being baptized into the idolatry of the *conquistadores*. The missionaries of this period played a significant role in the history of popular religiosity. Contrary to the popular political belief of the time, many missionaries believed the Indians to be human beings who had rights and deserved respect. Within this perspective, the missionaries devised a specific evangelization process.

The conversion of Mexico, for example, was entrusted to three mendicant orders: the Franciscans, the Dominicans, and the Augustinians. Many of these missionaries, confronted with Aztec beliefs, rituals, and feasts, took these cultural elements as the starting point for evangelization. As Enrique Dussel has demonstrated, a kind of proto-catechumenate was improvised by these missionaries, which in some cases incorporated Aztec customs into the conversion process. In these cases, the Gospel message was expressed in Indian terms, which allowed the neophytes to understand the teaching from their own cultural perspective. The spirituality of the mendicants, mixed with the spirituality of the Indians and expressed in Indian religious patterns, became an approach which many missionaries employed for preaching the Gospel.

In this context the missionaries also developed a process for baptism which was characterized by five steps: 1) proclamation of the Gospel; 2) a brief period of catechesis; 3) baptism; and 4) further catechesis; 5) with a living out of the new Christian way of life. We have evidence that certain sixteenth century reformers like the Dominicans Bartolomé de Las Casas and Antonio Montesino, as well as Bishop Vasco de Quiroga of Michoacán, employed such a process in their work among the Indians.[3] As is clear from the work of these particular missionaries, Christianity was not always imposed as an isolated belief system, but in some notable instances was conceived as a way of life springing from two great cultures: one Christian, the other Indian. It is true that the ministerial approach of Las Casas, Montesino and de Quiroga was a limited experiment, one not always fully appreciated by many of their contemporaries. The very fact that such an approach was even attempted, however, is important for us to acknowledge.

Having thus baptized the Indians, these missionaries hoped to form small Christian communities where people would live according to the "new way." It was presumed that it would take time for the baptismal experience to be integrated into the Indian culture, and consequently many of the "old ways" were allowed to coexist with the new. Unfortunately, for political and economic reasons this experiment was not allowed to continue. Since these new communities were not income-producing for the crown, this noble initiative was stopped and the incorporation process interrupted after baptism. Further catechesis and community building were confined to the obligatory rituals of the institutional church. Conditioned to adapting themselves to the requirements of their conquerors, the Indians maintained their Christian faith while secretly continuing with their traditional beliefs. But this time, mixed in with their traditional beliefs were the seeds of Christian faith and the treasures of the Gospel.

The past four hundred years have slowly witnessed the blossoming of these seeds and the opening of these treasures. There is a growing appreciation for all that we have been given. It would thus seem that the last step, envisioned by the missionaries, is finally coming to pass: the light of the Gospel is now restoring, purifying, and integrating popular religious customs into Hispanic Christian life through its worship.

THE VALUE OF POPULAR RELIGIOSITY

Hispanic teenagers live in two worlds. One is the world of Hispanic radio, food, music, dress, family relationships, and religious beliefs—which they call home. As soon as they leave this family dwelling, however, even though they might be living in a barrio, they become part of another world "in English," with its own dance rhythms, speech patterns, friends from a variety of racial and ethnic backgrounds, and certainly more critical ways of believing in God. This bi-cultural reality is well exemplified on those occasions when we encounter parents speaking to their children in Spanish and the children responding in English. The two worlds sometimes coexist, but often they tensely co-survive.

In the minds of many of the young, popular religious customs belong to the old ways of their parents, and need to be forgotten and replaced. As in other communities, Hispanic teenagers often find themselves on the periphery of religious life. It is their custom to stand in the church entrances on Sunday morning, "checking things out"—usually each other. Their place in the vestibule is actually quite symbolic of where they are with church and home at this time in their lives.

Yet, when the moment is right and these young Hispanics are faced with important life-decisions, suddenly "the old ways" are often accepted again as if they have never been laid aside. Marriages, baptisms, first communions must be celebrated with all of the popular customs of Hispanic religiosity in order to be right. Thus two worlds come together and again become one.

Our teenagers today face the perennial struggle for identity and self-esteem as they grow toward young adulthood. This struggle, however, is increasingly complicated by the individualistic tendencies which mark us as a nation. One extreme of our society is becoming a people of few and fewer personal interactions: where home video recorders replace the experience of a movie theater; television shopping by credit card eliminates the hassle of rubbing shoulders with another human being in a busy check-out line; and advances in computer technology enable us to telephone machines instead of people for information or services. Despite such "advances," however, there remains the very real need for the kind of human encounters that slowly and patiently give birth to authentic "I-Thou" relationships. The sharing of the human heart is not a fast food experience, but one which requires candlelight and music. The struggle for personal identity and self-esteem which teenagers face for the first time, and the rest of us wrestle with throughout our lives, is a journey of the heart which demands a heartfelt response. Worship which reflects the heart of a people, illuminating their gifts while acknowledging their limits, comforts and encourages us in this journey toward divine affirmation.

Here we begin to see, at least in a preliminary way, the value of popular religiosity. In large measure, popular religiosity responds to the affective side of religion and goes to the very heart of the individual and community. It is for this reason that popular religious customs and practices have endured some four hundred years in the Hispanic community and have been transported into new lands and cultures. They seem to give our lives a certain consistency and keep us on a steady course. They are the living symbols that touch us deeply. Therefore, what has been transplanted from across the border into this act of worship is not peripheral, but is the very heart of our people, and we seek to offer this heartful act of worship to others.

Implicit in this approach is a challenge to the individualistic values and tendencies of our society. Bishop Ricardo Ramirez of Las Cruces, New Mexico, calls this the "prophetic role" of Hispanic worship, in which customs of the dominant culture are questioned, given priorities are reevaluated, and absolutes are redefined. Worship is the act which highlights the criteria for evaluating society's influences, and which provides our people with the basis for incorporating other values into our lives.

Worship's potential for challenging contemporary values is

implicit in the *National Pastoral Plan for Hispanic Ministry* which acknowledges, for example, that the rejection of individualism is an important step in the evolution of a contemporary Hispanic spirituality.

> The III *Encuentro* process was yet one more step in the development and growth of their (Hispanic) spirituality. Many participants appeared to have moved from a personal and family spirituality to one that is communitarian and ecclesial. They moved from a sense of individual and family injustices to a recognition of general injustice to all people. This growth was sensed also in their awareness and experience of being in church, in their familiarity with ecclesial documents, in their active participation in liturgies and prayer. (#98)

Such growth in an ecclesial spirituality and communitarian sense of justice is undoubtedly related to a style of worship which defines and values the individual primarily in terms of the community.

We are a mestizo people, embodying the strengths and weaknesses of the Spanish and Indian cultures. Through this mixture of blood the faith practices of both have been interwoven. Yet the center of our life still revolves around the Indian belief in the Spirit. Our Indian ancestors believed that there were five great elements which constituted the world: earth, air, wind, fire, and the spirit who draws all life together. There is, consequently, no individual life but only the one life in which all living things share and struggle to live in harmony. This one Spirit gathers us together into community. And it is this Spirit who is at the center of popular religiosity for the Hispanic community.

It is this Spirit, now baptized, who touches the hearts of the people and engages them to live in harmony with God. God becomes "Diosito," a God of the home. God becomes "el Niño Dios" of Christmas, needing shelter and protection; and as an adult becomes the suffering Lord, tortured and crucified, who calls for our compassion. God is reflected in Mary: the mother, the grieving woman, and the good neighbor. God is also revealed in the lives of the saints, who are our constant companions and family. God weaves this Spirit around us in a thousand intimate and loving ways.

Touching the heart of a people means touching their spirituality in a tangible, visible way. It means bringing all of the happiness and pain, laughter and tears, joy and sorrow, to God in celebration. Sometimes such expression can be misinterpreted as emotional excess, financial extravagance, or simply an attempt at self-aggrandizement. Yet these apparent excesses are attempts to express the extremes in life experience: both the tragic and the ecstatic. They articulate a resounding "yes" to all that is, and all that can be. Some have called this the "fiesta approach" of popular religiosity: fiesta not in the minimalist sense of a party, however, but in the sense of gathering all of life's experiences into the embrace of the moment, be they filled with laughter or moved to tears.

Can't it be said that this is the true paschal mystery: the living, dying and rising of Jesus as he lives, dies and rises in this people? Can't it be said that this is the true Spirit of God set free within this people? Can't it be said that this is bringing the true faith of the people alive in this time and in this place?

The seeds of Christian faith present within our people were nurtured some four hundred years ago through a process of evangelization which is just now coming to fulfillment. And as these seeds come to fulfillment and blossom, so do they germinate hope for the future. Much of this hope is to be found in the new appropriation and appreciation of the traditional symbols of our people. It is not necessary always to create new symbols or new rituals. Sometimes hope is revived through the rituals and symbols which already exist, and which place us in contact with the Spirit of the world and the Spirit of Jesus, alive in his people. Such rituals and symbols, though adapted in their migration through time and space, nevertheless reappear from one generation to the next and continue to touch the heart of our people.

CHARACTERISTICS OF HISPANIC WORSHIP

El padrino awoke a little earlier than usual that Saturday morning. Today was the day. As he lay there, his mind wandered back to the dinner invitation which he had received several months earlier from José and María. He had wondered why they were so insistent on meeting for dinner, and so excited when the evening arrived. In the course of the meal the reason soon became clear. "When the baby is born, we want you to be *el padrino* and our *compadre.*" It was not so much a request as an expectation stemming from the long friendship which the three had shared. "But this is your first! Shouldn't some member of your family be asked?" "No," they insisted, "this is what both of us want!" Thus ended the discussion. And the morning had finally arrived. Today the baby would be baptized.

This would be an all day event. Relatives, traveling from as far away as California, had been arriving for days. The baptism was planned for 11:00 a.m., but that was just the beginning. Food still had to be cooked and prepared by the various friends and neighbors who had volunteered to help. Everyone would be expected to help decorate the hall. María had given *el padrino* special assignments, which included picking up the cake and the special meats from the neighborhood bakery. "Time to get moving," *el padrino* thought as he rolled out of bed.

Hispanic worship celebrates life and is centered around the sacraments. From the perspective of popular religiosity, these sacramental events help to focus on the true meaning of the life being celebrated. The four main sacramental events in the life of the Hispanic community are baptism, first eucharist, marriage, and that complex of rituals which accompany the death of an individual, sometimes referred to as "the sacrament of death and rising."

As for the other sacraments, confirmation is celebrated by many Hispanic families when the child is still very young— perhaps only two or three years old—and is not a major moment for celebration. This practice, however, is certainly changing as parents confront the practice in the United States of confirming teenagers. Penance still remains a private moment and is usually experienced as a preparatory step for receiving some other sacrament. Holy orders—due, in part, to the lack of Hispanic role models—still has not touched most of our families, though seeds of change are beginning to be sown here with each new wave of Hispanic permanent deacon ordinations and the increase in Hispanic vocational efforts.

It may be the baptismal story just related, however, which is the more typical experience in today's Hispanic community. Furthermore, such a story well demonstrates key characteristics of Hispanic worship. Though there are various ways in which these characteristics could be enumerated, it is possible to consider them under the six following headings.

Hispanic worship is **familial.** As illustrated by our baptismal story, worship is a time for the immediate and extended family of *compadres* to gather. On special occasions like baptisms or weddings, the inconvenience and expense of travel are secondary to the gathering of the family. It is not only on these special occasions that the family gathers for worship in the Hispanic community, however, for Sunday worship is a time for such gathering as well. Each Sunday of the year the church is transformed by the gathering community which takes possession of the building. The noise level noticeably increases as *saludos* and *abrazos* are exchanged between *compadres,* old friends, and new arrivals. Children make the aisles of the church their home as they look for ways to be entertained and cared for. Grandparents teach their grandchildren how the sign of the cross is made, how hands are to be folded and prayers are to be said. This is family as the first school of faith and the cornerstone of Hispanic worship.

Hispanic worship presumes a central role for **women.** It is especially the women of the community who are the traditional transmitters of faith through their example, their teaching, and their devotion. Further influenced by the lay leadership and feminist movements in the United States, Hispanic women are becoming even more visible in ministerial leadership. Where previously they were catechists, they are now directors of religious education; where previously they were sacristans, they are now lectors and ministers of communion; where previously they were helpful neighbors, they are now ministers to the sick and shut-ins. Hispanic women are the ones who know "the right ways" of praying for the dead, for celebrating *posadas* and for organizing feast days. They are the new found pastoral associates, leaders of liturgy teams, and directors of social ministry. And it is their link with tradition and vision for the future which is enabling new ways of faith to grow from the old ways.

Hispanic worship is the worship of the **young.** Sociologically, Hispanics are one of the youngest ethnic groups in the United States today. In a recent background report prepared for Pope John Paul II's 1987 visit to the United States, it was reported that the median age of the non-Hispanic population in the United States is 31.9 years, whereas the median age of Hispanics is 25.1 years. Attending to the youth element in our communities, however, does not necessarily mean resorting to teen or adolescent focused worship. Rather, we need to recognize the large number of parents who become grandparents by age forty, and great grandparents by age sixty. These relatively young and vital people become the "wise ones" in the parish and have the responsibility for nurturing the younger generations in the ways of our faith. For this they are revered and held in esteem by our community. As for the large numbers of children, adolescents, and young adults in our communities, their energy and enthusiasm is always a great promise and challenge to our worship. Conscious efforts must be made to invite them into full, conscious, and active participation in our worship and in the whole life of the church. Pastorally this suggests that our worship should be attractive and contemporary without being faddish or contrived.

Hispanic worship is characterized by a strong devotion to **Mary.** Though she has different titles in different countries, is often depicted in the dress of various regions and nationalities, and is honored by innumerable feasts and special days of devotion, she is yet for us the same woman. Mary is so identifiable because her life is so close to our own. She is poor, giving birth to a son in a stable. She is worried and anxious when the child is lost on a journey. She is the companion and follower of Jesus during his public ministry. She is the widow and grieving mother in need of consolation and comfort. She is the faithful woman who prays constantly. As with all the saints, but more than any other, she is our neighbor and friend: attentive to our worries and frustrations, supportive with her gentility and care, opening her hands and heart to us in prayer.

Hispanic worship is **musical.** Since music pervades all of life's experiences in the Hispanic community, it is natural that in our worship as well music should serve to weave our prayer together into a unified song of praise. Among our ancestors, music was a vehicle for expressing truth. Musical liturgy is for us a proclamation of Gospel truth in rhythm, melody, and text which brings the community to life. Though this phenomenon is universal in all of the Hispanic churches, the musical experience of the United States is quite different from that of the Latin or Caribbean countries. Here the guitar and percussion instruments have come to dominate, and there has been a definitive movement away from the dominance of the organ in our worship. Furthermore, in the United States more than anywhere else, melodies reminiscent of home feasts now resound through our churches. Hispanic people want to sing and willingly respond to the kind of musical leadership that invites them into the celebration.

Hispanic worship is an **embodied** experience. Life is lived in close quarters in our neighborhoods and in our homes. Houses pushed up against each other, apartment buildings overflowing with residents, and several families sharing cramped living quarters are not unusual experiences for us. Worship like life, therefore, means rubbing shoulders with each other just like at home. This means not only being touched at home and at prayer, but it also means being physically present to each other. It means an *abrazo* rather than a handshake, taking care of everyone's children in the church as if they were your own, and being in full contact with the symbols of life so that food, drinking, washing, and anointing are all savored to their fullness and felt more than just seen. It means that our celebrations are filled with flowers and candles, colors and incense, movement and texture and light. It means the close proximity of ministers to community and community to community. It means, therefore, the ability to be touched and the freedom to touch another human being in the presence of the holy.

All of these characteristics point to one simple fact about Hispanic liturgical life: Hispanic worship is people centered rather than ritual centered. It is the gathering of the community in song and celebration more than the proper execution of the rubrics which is at the center of our public prayer. Liturgy is for us not the proper reading of a book but a movement of the community's heart, seeking to express itself in one voice and in one living prayer.

THE INTEGRATION OF HISPANIC RITUALS AND
THE ROMAN LITURGY—SELECT EXAMPLES

"You start where the people are at," said the old priest to his newly ordained associate. "You should know that by now," he gently chided. The ministerial newcomer was truly embarrassed that his youthful enthusiasm had been so blind. He had only wanted to update the first communion Mass when he suggested eliminating the extra *padrinos*, candles, and arm bands which only complicated the liturgy. In doing so, however, he had walked over the land mines of people's feelings, transforming a rather tranquil get-together into a last minute showdown between himself, parents, and members of the pastoral staff. "You start where the people are at" would be engrained in his memory forever. The old man, in turn, smiled to himself remembering *his* first experience with the "golden rule," as he hurried to answer the phone.

Beginning where people are, and not where we want them to be, is an important "commandment" for any pastoral practitioner and an essential part of the evangelization process. More than a rule, however, such an awareness translates into a style of ministry that first seeks to experience the way people live. Where prayer is concerned, it means beginning with waiting, watching, and living the experiences of another's prayer. In so doing, the minister's own prayer becomes a source of reflection: past experiences of communal and individual prayer, as well as invitations to pray in new ways, can be more deeply appreciated. Eventually ministerial leadership, communal expression, and personal appreciation converge, giving rise to prayer forms which are enriched because of such convergence.

The genius of the Roman Rite is traditionally expressed in terms of its simplicity, clarity, and brevity. These characteristics were especially apparent when the rite was celebrated exactly the same all over the world. Since the Constitution on the Sacred Liturgy, however, has called us not only to adapt a few externals of the rite, but to strive to truly inculturate the worship into the various cultures of the world, we may have to rethink the nature of this rite's genius. Perhaps at the present time the Roman litury is best understood as a kind of skeleton which is recognizable as a human being, but an unnamed human being without a specific identity. It is not until it takes on the flesh and blood of a living culture that this rite comes to life and effectively calls us to life in Christ.

For this skeleton to be enfleshed by Hispanic culture means, therefore, celebrating in Spanish, but it also means much more than just an act of translation. Though it is undeniable that language is one of the most important expressions and vehicles of a culture, it is also clear that language is only one such element. Spanish alone, therefore, cannot transform a generic, all-purpose celebration into Hispanic worship. It is, instead, only by drawing upon the full repertoire of religious and cultural symbols—which means integrating the rituals of popular religiosity with official forms of worship—that true Hispanic worship will emerge. It is such an integration which we hope to represent here with a few select examples.

Posadas

The *posada* is a Christmas custom of the Mexican and Mexican-American communities which reenacts Joseph and Mary's search for an inn (*posada*) before the birth of Jesus. This ritual reenactment traditionally occurs outdoors as part of a novena which serves as a preparation for Christmas. The *posada* specifically consists of special hymns which are sung in dialogue between two groups of people: one outside representing Joseph and Mary, and another group inside representing the innkeepers. Lodging is denied to the pilgrims several times until, at last, they are joyfully invited into the home. Once inside, the assembled community prays a rosary and a litany, and then more hymns are sung. The evening usually concludes with special foods, refreshments and perhaps a piñata for the children.

The *posadas* are special plays which incarnate a Gospel story.

They are a lived prayer which young and old share together. In some places, because of the cold climate which prohibits an outdoor celebration, the church becomes the home for the community. In this adaptation the different vestibule doors become the inns, and the various roles are taken by different members of the parish family. The prayers on this night are led by the *rezadores* or those members of the community who know the hymns and special prayers by heart. It is possible to augment the ritual with short passages from the Gospel and perhaps a brief reflection by a catechist, deacon or priest. Doing so helps transform this traditional retelling of a quaint religious story into a revelation of the Spirit's presence among us. In some places small ecclesial communities which have formed in various neighborhoods make the *posadas* their own. Gathering inside the homes of the local faithful, children hold painted poles which now represent the doors of the inn. More emphasis is placed on proclaiming the word, as is characteristic of such neighborhood based communities, which helps underline the true significance of the coming feasts for the participating families.

On Christmas Eve the entrance rites of the eucharistic liturgy can become the last stage of the *posada*. The people gathered in the church sing the traditional hymns which again celebrate the journey of the pilgrims and joyfully open the doors of their hearts to welcome them once more. The Gospel is an invitation to be pilgrims as well, journeying to hear and see the living word. And in the end, all are led to another prepared fiesta: food and drink which manifest the incarnate gift of God, shared with all this Christmas Eve.

Related to the *posadas* is a special Puerto Rican custom called the *parrandas*. This ritual tradition begins just prior to Christmas and concludes on the feast of the Three Kings. Its own contribution of hymns, home visitations, and special foods also allows various familial traditions to be integrated with the ongoing celebration of the Christmas season, especially highlighting the feast of the Epiphany.[4]

Quince Años

The celebration of the fifteenth birthday in a young woman's life is a potentially important catechetical moment for her

21

family as well as for the other young people who celebrate with her. Conversely, however, perhaps no other Hispanic celebration has the same potential for eliciting such sharp criticism from priest and people alike as the *quince años*. The focus of such criticism is often the financial excess of these events in families of limited means, who nonetheless desire to provide a memorable celebration for the young woman. Despite the potential difficulties of this celebration, however, it is true that this family custom provides a rich opportunity for engaging the faithful and proclaiming the good news. Few works recognize this potential as well as Angela Everia's classic *La Quinceañera*, which discusses both the necessary catechesis prior to the celebration as well as the ritual of the day itself.

A proper celebration of *quince años* presumes a gathering of the participating young people beforehand. This gathering, which can take the form of a mini-retreat, is not primarily for the sake of input, but is a time of sharing. This is an ideal opportunity to encourage the young people to speak about their lives, their faith, and their doubts. It is also an opportunity to tell again the stories of how this custom originated, and what it can mean for us today. Such a gathering can allow the young to express their opinions about the church, and at the same time can challenge them to live their faith according to their customs and the call of the church. This vocational responsibility can be symbolized in the preparation of these youthful participants to be readers and singers, ministers of communion and welcomers at the approaching celebration. In another session the parents and perhaps the *compadres* of the *quinceañera* can be encouraged and guided to compose their own prayer of gratitude for the daughter and family. Such preparation can, in the short run, enable them to witness their faith at this celebration, and in the long run deepen their commitment to celebrate the ongoing proclamation of the Gospel in the midst of their family. Throughout this preparation of friends and family the young woman herself needs to reflect upon her developing Christian commitment to family and community as she takes this important step toward adulthood. She should be prepared, through personal reflection and dialogue with her family and pastoral team, to make an offering or contribution to the community. This is not meant to be a financial donation, but some gift of herself for the betterment of her family, her community, and herself, such as a commitment to finish her high school education or to become involved in teaching catechism to the children of the parish.

Like other sacramental moments, the ritual itself can be celebrated as a rite of passage: passage from childhood to adulthood, from passivity to participation, from recipient to giver. With parents and godparents at her side, surrounded by her friends, she is handed the candle lit from the Easter candle, renews her baptismal vows, clearly proclaims her offering, and signs herself with baptismal water. The *quinceañera* also receives Hispanic symbols of faith from the community—a medal of the Virgin, a prayer book, rosary, and a ring of promise—and she is affirmed as an example of the young in this parish who are willing to give more of themselves for the good of family and church.

Novenario

It is with an embrace and the words "Te acompaño en tus sentimientos"[5] that the consolation of grieving is begun. Death is an experience which we all share, and for the Hispanic community it is a special time where tears, *abrazos* and prayer all come together. It is a moment which everyone in the family and in the extended family shares—a time for food and drink provided in abundance by neighbors and friends. Everyone takes a turn. Everyone has a turn.

The rites provided by the church for the grieving process are a special opportunity for incorporating our heritage. The official ministers of the church along with the *rezador(a)* guide this process. The wake service, for example, could be structured around the recitation of the rosary which the *rezador(a)* leads. There are particular prayers at the end of each decade, and after the rosary a specific response to the Marian litany needs to be offered for the deceased. Integrating appropriate hymns and brief, litany length scriptural passages into this rosary service further enriches such traditional prayer with key elements of the church's official liturgy. Closing intercessions and a blessing of the body with holy water effectively bring the wake to a close while offering a ritual link to the funeral Mass itself.

Throughout the ritual process it is important to continue speaking the various names of the living and the dead who hold a special place in the heart of the grieving community. This includes naming the deceased, the dead relatives of the deceased, living family members, and all the patron saints, from that of the town where this life began to that of the church and cemetery where the earthly journey comes to an end. These are the names which will be remembered by the family, who will continue this prayer in the days and months ahead. An important focus during this prayer is the *altarcito*, a small altar which Hispanic families traditionally set aside as a special place of blessing and prayer. The picture of the deceased is enshrined here and a candle, entrusted to the family by a representative of the parish, can be lit during each prayer gathering.

For nine nights following the burial relatives and friends will gather in the family home for the *novenario*. The traditional content of this family novena is, again, the rosary and Marian litany, which are led by the *rezador(a)*. This custom of rosary and litany, however, can simply and effectively be combined with another traditional prayer, namely, vespers, which is the church's evening prayer of praise and intercession. Beginning at the *altarcito* with the lighting of the candle which was originally lit from the Easter candle and presented to the family at the funeral Mass, the *novenario* could then continue with a traditional Hisanic hymn like "Resucitó." The recitation of the rosary could provide the basic framework for the rest of vespers, employing the five decades of the rosary like the traditional five psalms of evening prayer. Each set of ten "Aves" could be concluded by selected verses from the psalms. The Marian canticle normally sung at vespers, that is, the Magnificat or "O María, Madre Mía," could easily follow. An abbreviated litany of intercession, concluding prayer and sign of peace would bring the service to a close. Such a novena of vespers could effectively combine the official prayer of the church with traditional Hispanic prayer and put both at the service of those who grieve.[6]

Each of these Hispanic traditions, the *posadas, quince años* and *novenario* are seasonal or occasional examples of the kind of cultural and liturgical integration which needs to occur not only at such special times but on the ordinary Sunday gatherings of the community. In some ways Sunday worship—like these specific examples—exists in a world of its own. With its own rules and rhythms, it is a somewhat spontaneous and constantly changing experience. Hispanic worship runs on its own time, namely, when the people have gathered rather than when the clock has struck the appropriate hour. It moves with the freedom of the dance and not always according to the prescribed plan and predetermined order. It has its own spirit which, when respected, bursts forth with an enviable vitality, but can be stifled or quenched by inflexible attitudes. Hispanic worship is not random or chaotic, but it is alive and responsive to the moment. Our adaptations should be similarly responsive.

SHAPING HISPANIC WORSHIP TODAY

Two Parables for Sunday Worship

Sunday Mass at Agua Bendita Parish is scheduled for noon, and with the striking of the hour the priest heads down the aisle with one of the two lectors and two out of three servers in tow (the other is quickly vesting and will catch up with the rest at the altar). Miraculously, the communion ministers came in together today. The choir is singing marvelously while the few people who are here on time are still searching through their books for the right page. Upon arriving at his chair, the priest begins Mass with the announcement that small children will be asked to follow two women into the sacristy for their own service. The toddlers leave hesitantly as their parents cast soulful glances at their departing offspring. Some parents refuse to send their children and hold them close. "At least now the noise level will be a bit more tolerable," muses the presider as the sacristy door finally closes. Mass continues with a welcome to all who have managed to arrive on time.

On the other side of town at Santa Ceniza Parish the choir continues rehearsing with the gathering people after the clock has struck twelve. Well-known melodies are recalled while new ones are taught, and a growing number of people find their way into the pews. There is a gradual warming in welcome and hospitality while the presider and ministers gather the children of various ages. With the music and singing now at full force, they begin to walk together down the aisle, children and adults, hand in hand. Everyone eventually finds a place in the sanctuary, on chairs, on the altar steps, or in a convenient pew, while the presider recalls the "old way" of making the sign of the cross: "Por la señal de la santa cruz . . . " Everyone joins in the well-known ritual. "Hand-in-hand liturgy," thinks the presider. "Oremos."

Speaking Spanish, singing with a guitar, and throwing a serape on an altar do not make Hispanic worship. Or, said another way, there is a difference between food from Taco Bell and a home cooked Mexican meal. One is impersonal and superficial whereas the other is familial and loving. Hispanic worship is prayer of the Hispanic home, and there are both similarities and differences from house to house, kitchen to kitchen, and tradition to tradition. Rice and beans, for example, are staples for almost all Hispanic groups. Yet rice and beans— sometimes served separately, sometimes served together—are seasoned in vastly different ways by the Puerto Rican, Cuban, Mexican, Guatemalan, Peruvian and various other communities which comprise the Hispanic reality. And it is precisely in entering the house and smelling the rice and beans in their own particular seasoning that we know what it is to be home.

Similarly, shaping Hispanic worship today means being aware of the general and specific ingredients which make up this ritual feast. There is, however, no recipe for successful worship. Rather, there are certain intuitions and valued perspectives, shaped by their contact with the Spirit who is present, which can blend people, word, and symbol into a living tradition of praise.

It should be evident by now that Hispanic culture has a deep respect for tradition, and Hispanic worship needs to do the same. Since the process of inculturation presumes a blending of traditions, however, one needs to respect both the liturgical traditions of the Roman Catholic Church and the cultural traditions of the Hispanic people. This means that a contemporary form of Hispanic worship in the United States cannot be achieved merely through some preset formula which mixes in equal parts Roman liturgy and traditional rituals, nor by uncritically incorporating every local custom into the community's worship. The process is much more complex than that and requires serious study, extensive experimentation, and critical evaluation. To aid in this ongoing process, we offer the following principles and cautions. It is our hope that in a preliminary way these might contribute to the important work of shaping Hispanic worship today.

It is important for us to note that although it is linguistically or politically expedient to refer to all Spanish speaking people as "Hispanic," the fact is that there are many ways of speaking Spanish, of baptizing a baby, of singing a hymn amongst our people. Hispanics are diverse. We pronounce our words differently, laugh at different jokes, and enjoy different foods. Yet in this diversity there is a fundamental mental unity, for we understand one another's experience of family, respect for tradition, and commitment to religious values.

Popular religiosity is a reality which encompasses innumerable rituals and a multitude of faith expressions which have almost as many meanings as interpreters. In our inculturation process it is important to explore the individual value and meanings which each ritual has in a particular community at this particular time. This is, unquestionably, a difficult process at first, attempting to discover the origin, history, and potential significance of traditional customs. These steps are necessary, however, if our adaptation is to be credible and appropriate. Furthermore, in this process of questioning and searching we find the roles of teacher and learner blurred or even reversed, and this common quest for understanding builds trust and charity.

The caution in recognizing this diversity in the Hispanic community is that this richness in a variety of traditions and perspectives should not be an excuse for or source of isolation and division between our people. In our struggle to respect the uniqueness of each national or regional group of Hispanics, we cannot allow ourselves to sacrifice solidarity on the altar of individuality. What irony if we allow ourselves to be a people divided despite our common traditions and language. Hopefully a truly catholic perspective will call forth unity in our diversity and enable us to move from crowd to community.

On the Centrality of the Family: Principle and Caution 2

It is not possible for us to overemphasize that Hispanic worship must involve the whole family. The consequence of this realization is that every kind of family member needs to be recognized in a way which boldly announces how valued and how important they are to the faith community. This requires that we explore every possibility for inclusivity in our ministries, striving at the same time to create a familial atmosphere for prayer.

Besides fostering the roles of various family members in existing ministries, we also need to support those ministries which have already emerged from the family and the home. The *rezador(a)*, or the one who knows the traditional ways of prayer, needs to be encouraged to assume leadership both in the family rituals and in the official worship. The *padrino* or *madrina* must be understood as more than just a sponsor or benefactor. They are companions who, if properly chosen and prepared, can actually guide their "child" in the ways of faith. If they can be nurtured as "life-guides," journeying with their godchild through each sacramental moment, they can become authentic and valuable witnesses to the entire faith community. Such new ministries, like the traditional liturgical, catechetical, and service centered ministries need to be encouraged—but encouraged not as clerical expansions but as natural out growths of family life and community needs. Such emphasis on family ministry, however, must not blind us to the challenge of divorce and separation which confronts us. The growing number of single parents need to be embraced by the extended family and invited into these ministries. Characteristically hospitable, the Hispanic family itself must learn to minister by holding these members close.

Another caution which stems from this focus on family ministries regards the possible diminishment or dismissal of the vital role of our priests and deacons. The call for new or evolving ministries, however, does not imply the eclipse of traditional forms of clergy but the need for new forms of cooperation with them. The ordained are an important part of the family of ministers who together are held in great affection.

Continuity with Baptism: Principle and Caution 3

Our baptismal rites embody a richness in theology and symbolism which can nourish us throughout our entire life. Christian worship in general and Hispanic worship in particular seem to spring from the rites of baptism. The continuous employment of candle, water, white garment, and other central symbols during the liturgies of first communion, confirmation, *quinceañera,* marriages, and funerals demonstrate how these simple signs can accompany us on our faith journey and reveal new meanings along the way. These externals, however, are only signs of the deeper process of commitment and conversion which hopefully accompanies the rituals. Our traditional attention to these recurring symbols, therefore, is an opportunity to engage the community in the continuous challenge of baptism.

The caution, however, is that baptism in the Hispanic community is very much a child centered event, and there are few adults among us who are engaged in the process of full initiation. Consequently, the baptismal imagery for many holds little challenge and remains a harmless and somewhat nostalgic evocation of an infancy ritual. Therefore we need to explore more aggressively the possibilities which the Rite of Christian Initiation of Adults holds for us. Here is a conversion process, punctuated by rites, which challenges us to a continuity not only of symbols, but more so of commitment and service. The RCIA is an important model for transforming unconnected, individual rituals into a pattern of life expressed in these rituals which invite us deeper into the mystery. In this light the post-baptismal rituals of adolescence need to be important evangelical moments when the Gospel is progressively heard more clearly and embraced more willingly.

The Use of Religious Artifacts: Principle and Caution 4

Besides the previously discussed symbols of baptism, Hispanic peoples frequently employ many other religious artifacts in their home and community worship. The continuous presence of rosaries and prayer books, medals and crucifixes, are tangible expressions of that chacteristic of Hispanic worship which we call "embodied." Such "sacramentals" are very important in our tradition and become the *recuerdo* or remembrance which literally allows the prayer event to be held in one's hands. The employment of such religious symbols must be respected and integrated into that larger reality we call liturgy. To the extent that such integration can occur, so to that same extent will we have informed our public worship by our cultural practices and enabled popular religious customs to shape the official prayer of the church.

The caution, of course, is that religious artifacts can easily become the focus of our rituals instead of the people who enact them. We have in the past succumbed to the allures of superstition which place power in objects instead of in the hands of God. As much as possible, however, we must check the spread of such magical notions. We are a sacramental church and consequently value religious artifacts as incarnational gifts, enabling us to encounter God through creation. It is important, however, to remember that things are not more important than people, and that creation is not an end in itself.

The Place of Music: Principle and Caution 5

Music stirs the heart in a way that nothing else can. It truly has a power and magic all its own. Music is unquestionably important in Hispanic worship, and we value engaging rhythms and inspiring texts which enliven our prayer. Happily we possess a core of traditional hymns which are liturgically appropriate during various seasons and on particular feasts. Popular songs like "Bendito, Bendito" and "De Colores" continue to hold a special place in our hearts and need to be integrated into our worship. There are also significant strides being made in the development of new Hispanic liturgical music in the United States, with such songs as "Danza del Ofertorio" by Rosas, "Dios te Salve María" by Sosa, and "Profetiza Pueblo Hispano" by Zárate. This new music, along with contemporary compositions from other countries like Gabaraín's "Pescador de Hombres" and our traditional songs and hymns, offers us a body of resources which almost could be considered a national repertoire of Hispanic liturgical music. Such a repertoire is an important component for sound Hispanic liturgy.

The development of such a repertoire, however, takes time. In the interim we learn by our mistakes. We must be cautious in determining that music for our worship is musically, liturgically, and pastorally appropriate. These criteria, spelled out in the episcopal document *Music in Catholic Worship*, can guide contemporary composers to write melodies that are as culturally identifiable as they are liturgically sound. Gratefully the tendency to employ such melodies as "Michael Row Your Boat Ashore" with a Spanish religious text is fast disappearing, as more worthy compositions are emerging.

31

CONCLUSION

Musings from under the Palm Tree

Just before light turned to darkness the three friends instinctively found themselves looking at one another. All of them, freshly molded by the same creative hand and breathing the same life-giving Spirit, pondered a similar thought. "We are so much alike as we await the setting of the sun: dreaming, wondering, hoping. There are endless possibilities ahead of us. Can we not help one another to fashion a new world? It is worth a try." And the Lord God, aware of what they were thinking, looked at them with love and said, "This is good!"

These words continue to ring out for all of God's people. They are the words which took flesh in Jesus, one like us in all things but sin. As a member of a human family and an ethnic community, he was shaped and fashioned by his culture. It was from this perspective that he saw the world, made decisions, and offered prayer. His words became Gospel truth, shattering false illusions of national supremacy and fostering unexplored bonds of human compassion and charity.

The Gospel of Jesus Christ does not canonize, but affirms and transforms all cultural hopes and dreams into authentic expressions of love for God and neighbor. What we share most is our humanity—a humanity molded in the image of God. We, as Hispanics, can turn to our sisters and brothers around us and value them as our trusted companions. We can be grateful for the invitation to sit under the palm tree, which is more than an invitation to relax. It is, moreover, an opportunity to marvel at creation and the chance to watch the sunset from an entirely new perspective.

We are all molded by the same creative hand and breath the same life-giving Spirit. Through our exploration of individual ethnic and religious traditions we can thus uncover a similar and unifying motivation: to be one with our God. In the sharing of our religious journeys we enhance each other's lives. In the appreciation of each other's faith we affirm the plan of creation. God can only say, again and again, "This is good."

Notes

[1] The use of exclusive language here is reflective of the story's tradition and not the author's perspective.

[2] Anscar Chupungco, *Cultural Adaptation of the Liturgy* (New York: Paulist Press, 1982) 3.

[3] For a detailed presentation of the work of these and other reformers, see Robert Ricard, *The Spiritual Conquest of Mexico* (Los Angeles: University of California Press, 1966 [1933]); also Laurette Sejourne, *América Latina I: Antiquas Culturas Precolombinas* (Madrid: Siglo XXI de España Editores, S.A., 1971); and Richard Konetzke, *América Latina II: La época colonial* (Madrid: Siglo XXI de España Editores, S.A., 1972).

[4] For further examples of traditional Christmas customs, see "Latin American Customs of Advent and Christmas," *Liturgy 80* (November/December 1987) 7.

[5] "I am with you in your grief."

[6] For a fuller treatment of this ritual, see *Novenario por los Difuntos* (Chicago: Liturgy Training Publications, 1987), which we prepared for publication.

A SELECT ANNOTATED BIBLIOGRAPHY

Actualidad Litúrgica. Buena Prensa, Apartado M-2181, 06000 México, D.F.
 This is a bimonthly liturgical journal containing articles from around the world, as well as exegetical comments on the Sunday readings, suggested homilies, and model intercessions. It is a valuable, up-to-date resource.
Chupungco, Anscar. *Cultural Adaptation of the Liturgy.* New York: Paulist Press, 1982.
 A primer for initiation into the basics of liturgical adaptation. It situates this topic within the context of the Constitution on the Sacred Liturgy and the historical development of the Roman liturgy.

Elizondo, Virgilio. *Christianity and Culture.* San Antonio: Mexican American Cultural Center, 1975.

This classic work, in its third printing, is one of the first attempts to theologically address the Mexican American experience by a Mexican American.

Elizondo, Virgilio. *Galilean Journey.* New York: Orbis Books, 1983.

The author continues to address the Mexican American experience, now from the Galilean experience of Jesus.

Eagleson, John and Philip Scharper, eds. *Puebla and Beyond.* Maryknoll: Orbis Books, 1979.

This is a compendium of insightful commentaries on the Latin American Episcopal Conference of Puebla, Mexico (1979) by various authors. The text includes the major addresses of John Paul II at Puebla as well as the official translation of the final Puebla document.

Erevia, Angela. *Quinceañera.* San Antonio: Mexican American Cultural Center, 1980.

This eminently practical, bilingual booklet outlines the history of the *quinceañera* and further provides a penance service, catechetical instruction, two rituals, and a homily related to this event.

Galilea, Segundo. *Religiosidad Popular y Pastoral Hispano-Americana.* New York: Northeast Catholic Pastoral Center for Hispanics, 1981.

Popular religiosity is part of the pastoral spiritual reality for Hispanics in the United States. In a concise but detailed way this booklet offers a clear understanding of this theme.

Kirk, Martha Ann. *Dancing with Creation.* Saratoga, California: Resource Publications, Inc., 1983.

Martha Ann Kirk has provided an insightful reflection on embodied prayer, which she considers to be a spiritual discipline that enriches the spiritual life.

Konetzke, Richard. *America Latina II: La época colonial.* Madrid: Sigo XXI de España Editores, S.A., 1972.

A well written book on the colonization of the Americas by the Spanish and Portuguese, this work analyzes the conquest of the Americas in light of the current events in Europe.

Kraft, Charles. *Christianity in Culture.* New York: Orbis Books, 1984.

This substantial work is written for career missionaries by a missionary turned professor. Combining a biblical approach with reflections from his own experience, the author demonstrates how one can view the world from a cross-cultural perspective.

Maldonado, Luis. *Génesis del Catolicismo Popular.* Madrid: Ediciones Cristiandad, 1979.

Concentrating on a single period in history, Maldonado explores the genesis of popular catholicism in the Middle Ages.
Maldonado, Luis. *Religiosidad Popular*. Madrid: Ediciones Cristiandad, 1975.

Employing an anthropological perspective, this book describes Spanish festival times according to the various seasons of the year, offers interpretative keys for understanding these events, and demonstrates how popular religiosity can be united with the liturgy.

National Pastoral Plan for Hispanic Ministry. United States Catholic Conference of Bishops, 1987.

This important document, approved by the American bishops, outlines their concerns and hopes for Hispanic ministry in the United States today.

Paul VI. *On Evangelization in the Modern World*.

Issued on 8 December, 1975, this apostolic exhortation focuses not only on the nature and need for evangelization but also on the content and methods of evangelization, making it one of the most important official documents of its kind for the contemporary church.

Phase. Centro de Pastoral Litúrgica. Canuda, 45-47, Barcelona 2, Spain.

This is a scholarly bimonthly pastoral liturgical journal from Spain. Its various writers offer in-depth articles on a specific liturgical theme or topic for each issue.

Ramírez, Ricardo. *Fiesta, Worship and Family*. San Antonio: Mexican American Cultural Center, 1981.

This booklet is a collection of articles on the role and contribution of Hispanics to the United States and the Catholic Church.

Ricard, Robert. *The Spiritual Conquest of Mexico*. Los Angeles: Uniiversity of California Press, 1966 (1933).

This translation of the original French work provides a study of the apostolate and evangelizing methods of the mendicant orders in New Spain in the sixteenth century.

Sejourne, Laurette. *América Latina I: Antiguas Culturas Precolombinas*. Madrid: Siglo XXI de España Editores, S.A., 1971.

This scholarly work explores ancient pre-Colombian culture in Latin America.

Steware, C. Edward. *American Cultural Patterns*. Chicago: Intercultural Press, Inc., 1972.

The objective of this book is to supply a perspective on cross cultural patterns for those who work outside the United States. It highlights the differences in thought patterns, assumptions, and values held by people from the United States and people of other countries with whom they work.